Castles

C O N T E N T S

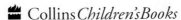
Collins *Children's Books*
Copyright © HarperCollins Publishers Ltd 1996

Castle Design

When you build a sandcastle on the beach you dig a circular ditch and throw sand into the middle to make a little hill. A thousand years ago, the first castles were built in just the same way. A strong timber wall was built inside the ditch. The area inside the wall was called the bailey and the hill was called the motte.

Stone keep
On top of the motte was a keep in which the lord and his family lived. Early keeps were wooden and burned easily, so later keeps were built of stone.

Concentric circles
Castle builders knew that walls kept out the enemy – so they designed castles enclosed by a series of stone walls. Impressive gatehouses were built into the walls.

Gatehouse

Eggs for his lordship

Fortified towns

By the middle of the 14th century, castles had developed into enormous and complicated citadels, often big enough to contain a whole town inside their walls. People who lived in the town laboured for the lord of the castle: providing him with food supplies, or working as servants or soldiers.

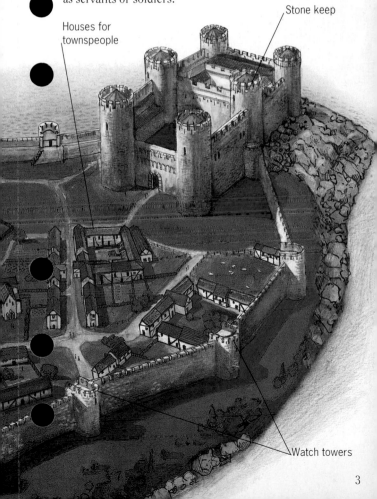

Stone keep

Houses for townspeople

Watch towers

Castle Mania

In 1066 Norman soldiers from France, led by William the Conqueror, invaded England. They crossed the Channel to England and defeated King Harold at the Battle of Hastings. On Christmas Day William was crowned king of England.

WILLIAM THE CONQUEROR

The porta-castle

William's army landed at Pevensey with sections for a prefabricated timber castle. It was put up and ready for use within 24 hours of landing. The army used the ruins of a Roman fort as the basis for the castle.

Let's talk tactics

William's strategy was to move forward, build a castle... move forward again, build another one. This meant he couldn't be attacked from behind and he could always retreat to a safe place. To save time he built wooden motte-and-bailey castles, rebuiding them in stone as soon as he could.

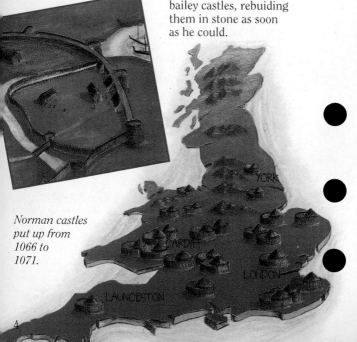

Norman castles put up from 1066 to 1071.

YORK

CARDIFF

LONDON

LAUNCESTON

THE FEUDAL SYSTEM

William, as king of England, was head of the feudal system. He put 200 barons who had come with him from Normandy in charge of large estates.

The barons ruled over their little empires and had several castles. But they had to promise to be loyal to the king and to raise troops for him.

The barons gave some land (often with a castle thrown in) to their knights. In return, the knights had to be ready to lead armies for the king.

Knights broke up their land into even smaller plots which they leased to serfs. In return, serfs had to work without wages, serve as soldiers, and pledge total obedience.

The Tower of London
The main feature of a Norman castle was its huge stone keep. Many are still standing today. The best-known is the White Tower, the heart of the Tower of London, built by William the Conqueror in 1081.

KEEP UP OR ELSE!

The number of castles built by William the Conqueror is incredible. Five years after the invasion he had already built 33. By the time he died, in 1087, he'd built at least 86.

Phew!

He was fast. He once built a castle in York in just eight days.

He was ruthless. To build his castle in Lincoln, he simply destroyed 166 homes that were in the way.

Crusader Castles

At the same time as William the Conqueror was bringing England under his control, Turkish Muslims invaded the Holy Lands. They captured Jerusalem and killed the city's Christian pilgrims. In 1095 the Pope called for a Holy War – a Crusade – to win back the Holy Lands.

CRUSADER ROUTES FROM EUROPE TO THE HOLY LANDS

Castle know-how

The Crusades lasted for 200 years, so the Crusaders learned a lot about building castles. They discovered how useful it was to have crenellations – those tooth-shaped tops to castle walls which protected archers from enemy arrows. They learned that castle walls should have towers at regular intervals to make them stronger and easier to defend.

SPOILS OF WAR

Crusaders who were lucky enough to get home again brought with them all sorts of things that had never been seen in Europe before (you can see some of them below). They returned with new knowledge they had gathered from Muslim doctors, astronomers and mathematicians. They even brought back a new game called chess.

LEMONS

SILK

GLASS

SPICES

If a knight died in battle, the figure carved on his tomb would have had crossed feet.

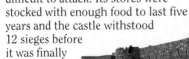

Battling monks

Some Crusaders were also monks. The Knights Templar took their name from a temple in Jerusalem. Over 20,000 of them died fighting in the Crusades. The Knights Hospitaller ran hospitals built along the Crusader routes to care for wounded soldiers and pilgrims.

Krak des Chevaliers

This mighty Crusader castle was built in Syria by the Knights Hospitaller. Standing on top of a hill, it was very difficult to attack. Its stores were stocked with enough food to last five years and the castle withstood 12 sieges before it was finally captured by the Muslims in 1271.

World Castles

Powerful rulers from many different civilisations built castles around the world to protect themselves.

Ancient keep

The oldest known stone castle is the keep at Doué la Fontaine on the banks of the River Loire in France. It dates back to the 10th century.

Underground castle

Between World War I and World War II, the French built a 1,000km long underground fortress along their border with Germany. Called the Maginot Line, it was designed to prevent German troops from ever being able to invade France again. It failed.

Inca fortress

Machu Picchu was an Inca fortress city. The Inca empire flourished in South America during the 15th century. Built high in the Andes mountains, the ruins of the great fortress of Machu Picchu were not discovered until 1911.

Spanish stronghold

The impressive Alhambra is one of the castles built by the Moors after they conquered Spain in the 13th century. The Alhambra covers 14 hectares of ground and is surrounded by massive walls.

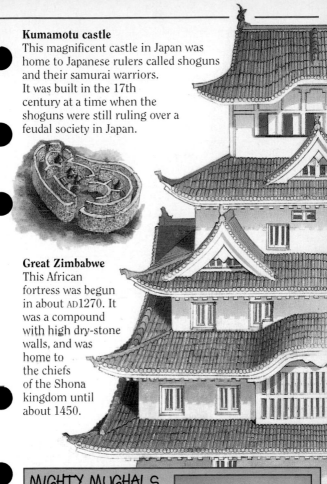

Kumamotu castle

This magnificent castle in Japan was home to Japanese rulers called shoguns and their samurai warriors. It was built in the 17th century at a time when the shoguns were still ruling over a feudal society in Japan.

Great Zimbabwe

This African fortress was begun in about AD1270. It was a compound with high dry-stone walls, and was home to the chiefs of the Shona kingdom until about 1450.

MIGHTY MUGHALS

The Mughals ruled a vast empire in India for three centuries. As their power weakened towards the end of the 18th century they retreated to the magnificent Red Fort in Delhi which was their last stronghold.

All in a Day's Work

As castles became bigger and more complex over the years, they took a lot longer to build. Caernarvon castle took 45 years and was never completely finished!

Medieval builders used a kind of crane that was actually a pulley turned by a man walking inside a treadwheel. Larger blocks of stone and heavy timbers were hauled up on these pulley systems.

As the wall grew, labourers toiled up ladders and ramps with baskets of stone on their backs.

Thick brick
A castle wall might be anything from two to six metres thick. It had inner and outer skins of great stone blocks cemented together with lime mortar. The space between was filled with rubble.

Supremos of stone

Masons were the men who cut and shaped stone. They were the most-respected and highest-paid members of the workforce. Master masons were experts in castle design. They travelled abroad to pick up new building techniques. Freemasons were 'free' because they were too skilled to be serfs. They were proud of their work and often 'signed' buildings with their own marks.

An army of workers

It took over 2,500 men to build Beaumaris Castle in 1295. Armies of tradesmen and labourers plus vast supplies of stone and timber were needed for any castle.

BLACKSMITH

CARPENTER

CARRIER

DOGSBODY

TOOLS OF THE TRADE

CARPENTER'S ADSE

CARPENTER'S BRACE

FRAME SAW

MASON'S MALLET AND CHISEL

NAILS

AWL

CONDEMNED

The Countess of Bayeux had a castle built for her by an architect called Lanfred. When she saw the finished building, she was so pleased that she had Lanfred executed on the spot, so that he wouldn't build such a splendid castle for anyone else. Nice to be appreciated!

Castle Protection

Castles surrounded by water were difficult to attack. Many castles were built on islands in natural or artificial lakes, others had deep moats dug around them. A heavily-

defended gatehouse equipped with a drawbridge was another essential high-security feature for any castle.

First the bad news...
Wrongdoers were dunked in the moat, sitting on a ducking stool. This was especially nasty if the castle had lavatories that emptied into the water!

... and now the good news!
The moat or lake was often well-stocked with fish, eels, ducks, swans and herons. They all belonged to the lord of the castle, but sometimes he granted fishing rights to pregnant women.

First the drawbridge...
If you were attacking a castle, you'd have to get across the drawbridge. Of course it was usually kept closed but even if it was down you might fall through a hidden trapdoor built into it or be struck down by arrows.

...Then the portcullis
The next obstacle for the enemy was the portcullis – a huge wooden grid with iron spikes that could be dropped down on attackers.

Caught in the courtyard!
The portcullis opened onto a small courtyard. If the attackers got this far they would be bombarded by arrows while stones and boiling oil rained down on them through murder holes above their heads.

MURDER HOLE

PORTCULLIS

DRAWBRIDGE

DRAWBRIDGE DESIGN

1

2

1 Drawbridges worked like huge seesaws. To open the drawbridge, the weighted end would drop down into a pit and the other side would lift up.
2 More elaborate versions had an upper lever attached to the bridge by chains.

Knight Attire

The fighting men who attacked and defended castles needed to be dressed and armed for the job. Each knight had to provide his own armour, weapons and warhorse.

Well-ironed!

Suits of armour had to be flexible. They were made from separate iron plates, joined together by rivets or leather straps.

1   2   3   4

Step-by-step dress

1 Padded under garments and 'arming doublet' (a jacket with leather laces).
2 Breastplate and leg armour laced to doublet.
3 Backplate and arm guards fitted to doublet.
4 Gauntlets (armoured gloves) and helmet put on.

Helmet

Breast-plate

Sword

Thigh shield

Shin pads

HERALDRY

Important families each had their own special badge called a coat of arms. This was passed down from generation to generation. If a lord and lady married, the coats of arms of both their families would be combined to create a new design.

CHAIN MAIL

The first knights wore suits of chain mail. These could have thousands of small, linked, iron rings. Later, shorter coats of chain mail were worn underneath solid plates of armour.

 1 Thick iron wire is bent into a ring.

3 Both ends are flattened and pierced.

2 Both ends of ring are overlapped.

4 The rings are fixed with metal rivets.

Trademarks

Making armour was a highly-skilled job. Armourers took pride in their work and often stamped the finished suits with special hallmarks.

Bodkin
A sharp bodkin point was more likely to pierce armour and wound the enemy if it was first smeared with beeswax.

Weighs a ton!
A suit of armour weighed about 20 to 25kg, so a fully-armed knight would be very heavy and very hot!

FRIEND OR FOE?

When knights rode into battle, they wore tunics and carried shields and banners which were all decorated with their coat of arms. That way they could tell friend from foe.

On the Attack

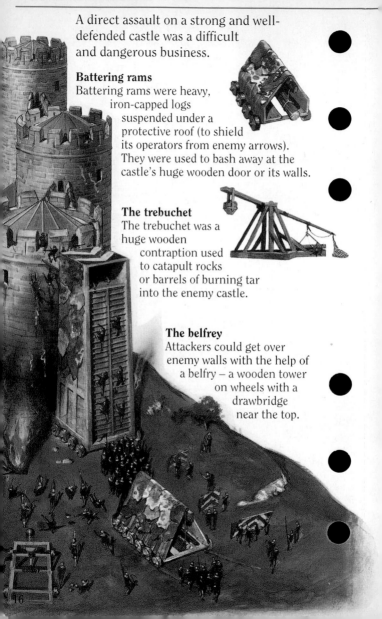

A direct assault on a strong and well-defended castle was a difficult and dangerous business.

Battering rams
Battering rams were heavy, iron-capped logs suspended under a protective roof (to shield its operators from enemy arrows). They were used to bash away at the castle's huge wooden door or its walls.

The trebuchet
The trebuchet was a huge wooden contraption used to catapult rocks or barrels of burning tar into the enemy castle.

The belfrey
Attackers could get over enemy walls with the help of a belfrey – a wooden tower on wheels with a drawbridge near the top.

Longbows
A skilled archer could fire up to 12 arrows per minute, shooting them to wound or kill an enemy soldier or cavalry horse over 300m away.

Greek fire
This lethal burning mixture of quicklime, sulphur and oil was always dreaded because it could not be put out with water.

Crossbows
Crossbows had to be loaded mechanically but the bolts they shot would travel even further than longbow arrows.

Loose cannons
The earliest cannons, used in the 14th century, were very dangerous to operate. They sometimes blew up when they were fired, killing the gunners.

UNDER OR OVER?
Tunnellers dug underneath the castle walls, replacing the earth and rock they removed with wooden props. They then set fire to the props. When the tunnel collapsed, it brought down part of the castle wall with it and the attackers could storm in.

Mangonel
The mangonel was a catapult powered by twisted ropes. Although it was less accurate than the trebuchet, it had a longer range and could smash rocks against castle walls.

17

Defending a Castle

A castle's main defence was its massive stone walls. From behind these walls, defenders used a grizzly array of tactics to crush their attackers. Many castles had concentric walls, getting higher towards the centre.

Wooden hourds stuck out from the top of the walls so defenders could drop rocks or firepots onto the attackers.

Firepots were full of burning tar – very nasty!

Grappling irons could grab the end of a battering ram to stop it bashing down the door.

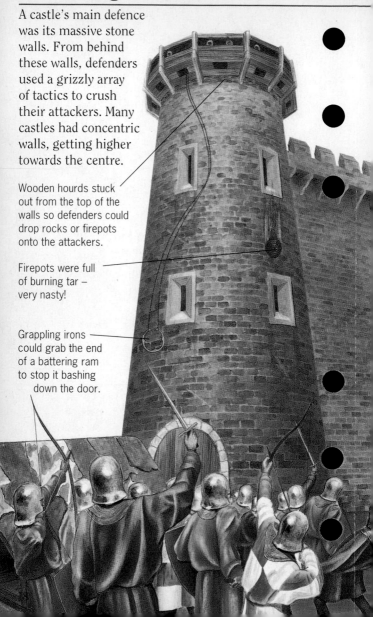

Machicolations
Some castles had permanent structures like hourds but made from stone instead of wood. They were called machicolations.

Narrow for arrows
Loops were the narrow slits in castle walls, designed to protect defenders while they poured arrows and crossbow bolts down on the attackers. Some loops were simple slits, others were shaped like crosses.

Early warning
Defenders put dishes of water on the floor as mine detectors and watched for ripples. Sometimes they dug counter-mines to meet the attackers' tunnel and fight it out underground.

My advantage!
Spiral staircases wound round to the right as they rose. This gave an advantage to the defenders: attackers trying to fight their way up would have less room to use their swords. Unless, of course, they were left-handed!

OH POOH!
Human excrement rained down on attackers fairly frequently. Okay, so it didn't kill you, but you tended to smell pretty disgusting.

Siege and Survival

If you weren't in a hurry, laying siege to a castle was safer and easier than attacking it. You simply had to surround the castle and wait for starvation, thirst or disease to force the castle to surrender.

Early germ warfare

A very nasty besiegers' trick was to lob bodies of people who had died of the plague into the castle. Or sometimes they used the heads of captured defenders.

Bird battle

Besieged castles would try to send messages by carrier pigeon. Attackers sent falcons after the pigeons to kill them in the air.

Siege tower

Attackers put up siege towers out of the range of arrow-shot, but close enough to see what people in the castle were up to.

Animal round-up
Before a siege the herds of sheep and cows would be brought within the castle walls to graze. The castle dwellers also raised pigs, peacocks, geese, swans and chickens for food – after all, why die of hunger?

Bee sweet
In medieval times people used honey, not sugar, as a sweetener. Castle bees were kept in straw hives tucked in between the crenellations.

Stocked up
Meat and fish were salted or smoked and stored in barrels. Supplies of grain, salt, onions and apples were on hand all year round.

Fresh water
A well was essential for siege survival. Defenders would guard it closely from enemy sabotage.

Well-armed
Your castle also had to be stocked up with weapons and missiles of all sorts.

TIME FOR A TREATY
Sieges could be brought to an end by making a deal. In Europe there was a '40-day rule'. If after 40 days the besieged castle had not been rescued by friendly troops, the defenders could surrender without disgrace or punishment.

21

Food and Feasting

Feasting was a serious business. Starting around 10am, it lasted well into the afternoon. If the king was present, he would sit at the high table.

Cheers!

Water was often foul and dangerous to drink so people drank ale and wine, even at breakfast.

Trenchers

Food was served on trenchers – thick slices of bread that soaked up the sauces.

Cutlery

Forks hadn't been invented in Medieval times, so people had to use fingers, a knife or, if they were lucky, a spoon!

OH NO... IT'S THE KING AGAIN

When King John decided to spend the Christmas of 1206 at Winchester, he sent an advance order for:

X1,500

X5,000

X20

X100

X100

Chaos in the kitchen

Castle kitchens were noisy, crowded places. Women weren't allowed anywhere near the kitchen and the cooks often worked naked because the heat from the ovens was unbearable. As the men worked, boys ran among them dishing out ale and water.

TODAY'S MENU

HORRIBLE PORRIDGE

STALE BREAD

A ROTTEN APPLE

PUTRID MEAT

Give us our daily bread

Lavish banquets were few and far between. On most days castle rations were more likely to be a chunk of meat pickled in salt water, a bowl of barley porridge, a slab of coarse bread and a wrinkled apple.

Dying to taste it!

The upside for the food taster was that he got to taste each dish before the king did. The downside was that if it was poisoned he died.

WHAT A JOB!

The ale conner had the job of testing the purity of beer. He had to sit in a pool of ale for half an hour. If the ale was too sugary, his leather britches would stick to the bench and the poor man would be very embarrassed when he stood up!

23

Highlife

Castle entertainments ranged from fairs to lavish jousting tournaments. And even if there was nothing planned, there was always the chance of a passing troupe.

Hunting
Medieval lords and ladies were mad about hunting and they'd hunt anything that moved: deer, wolves, hares and wild boar.

Falconry
Any lord would prize his hunting birds very highly. He would rarely be without a falcon tied to his wrist.

Jousting
Knights could show off their skills by challenging each other to a joust. The aim was to knock your opponent from his horse using a wooden lance.

That's entertainment

Castles were often visited by travelling entertainers. There were minstrels, jugglers, actors and puppet shows. And wandering musicians sang popular ballads of the day.

Joking jesters

A castle banquet would not be complete without the antics of a jester.

Grizzly

Bears still roamed the forests in Medieval Britain. Some were taken into captivity and led miserable lives entertaining the crowds as a dancing bears, or being forced to fight dogs in the cruel sport of bear baiting.

FOOTBALL MANIA

Football was such a wild and violent game in those days that King James I of Scotland had to ban this unruly sport from his castles!

Lowlife

For most people living in a Medieval castle, life was pretty tough. The whole place was dark and smelly, the food was usually off, your clothes were dirty and flea-ridden, and you never got a good night's sleep.

Bath time

Drawing water from the well and heating it in a furnace was such a performance that even royalty bathed only once every three weeks!

Castle conveniences

Castle lavatories were called garderobes. Some stuck out from the walls and emptied straight into the moat. Others drained into a cess-pit down an evil-smelling chute. The lord's family used a private garderobe. What's more, they had strips of cloth to wipe their bottoms. Everyone else had to make do with dried grass!

POSH   ORDINARY

From highlife to lowlife

1 The solar (furnished living quarters for the lord's family).
2 The garderobe.
3 Feasting and entertaining took place in the great hall.
4 Castle ladies spent much of their time in the spinning room.
5 The chamber where the lord and his courtiers held meetings.
6 Storerooms for food supplies.
7 Rooms for weaving cloth on the loom and making clothes.
8 The laundry.
9 Carpenters cut the timber and made wooden tools.
10 The joiner carved castle furniture in his workshop.
11 The blacksmith and farrier worked together in the smithy.
12 'Ale-wives' working in the brewery.
13 The potter at his wheel.
14 Wheelwright in the yard.

GONG PONG!

'Gong farmers' were the unlucky people who had to empty the cess-pits.

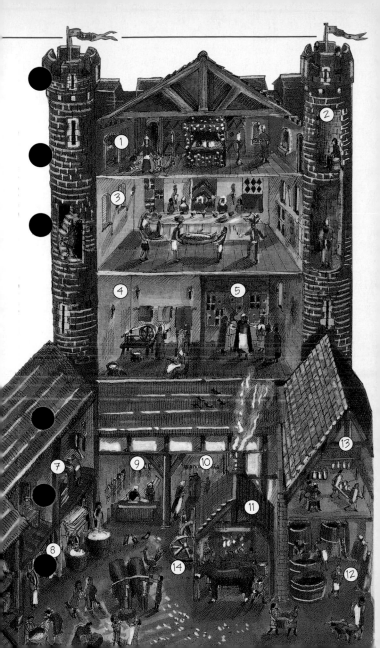

Gruesome!

Dungeons were dark, cold, filthy places. Prisoners spent years chained to the walls, with the threat of torture or death always hanging over them.

PILLORY
Minor crimes, like selling stale beer, were punished by the pillory. Passers-by would chuck rubbish at the trapped offender.

Oubliette
Very unlucky prisoners were shoved into this tiny cell, too small to move in, and left to rot away in agony until they died.

Pressing
Being slowly crushed to death was a horrible way to die. The torturer would add more weights every day.

Branding
Thieves were branded – marks were burned onto their faces or hands with red-hot irons

ROYAL RANSOM
Rich or royal prisoners were often kept in luxury – and were treated like honoured guests. They would be set free if family or friends raised enough money for a ransom.

PRISON CASTLE
In World War II the Germans used Colditz castle for Allied prisoners.

Hung...
Hanging on the gallows was a slow and painful death.

...and quartered!
Finally, the criminal's body was chopped into pieces.

...drawn...
The executioner cut open the prisoner to pull out his heart. The aim was to hold it up before the victim's eyes while he was still alive.

The rack
This torture was reserved for traitors. It pulled apart their joints slowly and painfully.

29

Follies and Fantasies

By 1500, the age of great castles was coming to an end. Castles were no longer built for defence, but fairy-tale castles were put up as fashionable homes for the rich.

Mickey Mouse's castle

'Mad King' Ludwig of Bavaria built a fantastic fairy-tale castle perched on high mountain crags. Bristling with crazy ornamental turrets, Neuschwanstein inspired Walt Disney's castles.

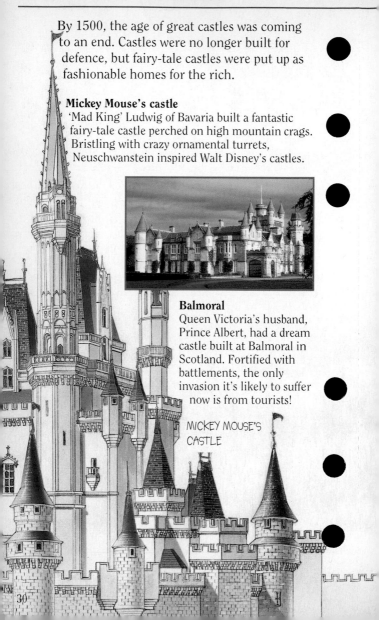

Balmoral

Queen Victoria's husband, Prince Albert, had a dream castle built at Balmoral in Scotland. Fortified with battlements, the only invasion it's likely to suffer now is from tourists!

MICKEY MOUSE'S CASTLE

A SUPER SOUVENIR

The American dream

William Randolph Hearst was a successful American media tycoon. He owned a number of newspapers and lived in luxury in a castle built for him in California.

A CASTLE FIT FOR A GROCER!

A man called Julius Drewe made his fortune from a chain of grocery stores and built himself Castle Drogo overlooking a steep valley in Devon.

Designer rubble

In the past, the gentry built fake castle ruins to add a bit of instant 'history' to their country estates.

Dracula's castle?

Count Dracula may have been based on a real historical prince, Vlad the Impaler, who lived in this castle in Romania. His enemies were put to death by having a wooden stake driven through their heart.

VLAD THE IMPALER

31

INDEX

First published in 1996 by HarperCollins
Children's Books,
A Division of HarperCollins Publishers
Ltd, 77-85 Fulham Palace Road,
London W6 8JB
ISBN: 0 00 197908 6

Illustrations: Siena Artworks, London
and Jane Gerwitz

Photographs: Bibliothèque International/
Portfolio Pictures 20; Bruce Coleman
Limited /Andy Price 8; Fotomas Index 24;
Hulton Deutsch Collection 4, 31;
©Michael Holford 7c, 9; Robert Harding
Picture Library 30, /©Adam Woolfit 7b,
12; Zefa 5.

A CIP record for this book is available
from the British Library

Printed and bound in Hong Kong